AmeRícan

by

Tato Laviera

Arte Público Press

Houston

AmeRícan is made possible by grants from the National Endowment for the Arts, a Federal Agency and the New York State Council on the Arts.

Arte Público Press
University of Houston
452 Cullen Performance Hall
Houston, Texas 77204-2004

Cover art courtesy of Juan Sánchez, "Plebicite," 1990.

Laviera, Tato.
    AmeRícan / by Tato Laviera.
        p.   cm.
    ISBN 1-55885-395-2 (pbk. : alk. paper)
    1. Puerto Ricans—Poetry. 2. New York (N.Y.)—Poetry.
I. Title.
PS3562.A849A44 2003
811'.54—dc21   2003044427
                                                           CIP

∞ The paper used in this publication meets the requirements of the American National Standard for Information Sciences—Permanence of Paper for Printed Library Materials, ANSI Z39.48-1984.

Printed in the United States of America.

3 4 5 6 7 8 9 0 1 2   10 9 8 7 6 5 4 3 2 1

CONTENTS

AmeRícan

Ethnic Tributes

Values

I. Pueblo

II. Nuyoricans

III. Rituals

Politics

Celebrating Life: The AmeRícan Poet Tato Laviera

After La Carreta Made a U-Turn (1979) and *Enclave* (1981), *AmeRícan* is Tato Laviera's third book of poetry. It speaks for the perspicacity of Arte Público Press that all three came out from the same publishing house.

Even more than the two preceding volumes, this is a book of affirmation and definition. The need for both seems obvious to anyone living in New York City. It may look still more urgent to a Black Puerto Rican New Yorker who happens to be one of the very fine poets of his group, a true spokesman. With *AmeRícan*, Tato Laviera confirms his excellent reputation as a vital poet and humanist. Laviera is postulating and "defining the new america, humane america" ("AmeRícan"), but he will not be absorbed by a mythical melting pot. His poem "asimilao" is one engaging, extended joke and a counterattack against those who want to see the New York Puerto Ricans as traitors to their culture. Speaking in the same direction, towards elements of an (often enough "Americanized") classist island attitude, Laviera formulates a plea in "nuyorican":

> yo me peleo por ti, puerto rico, sabes . . .
> y tú
> me desprecias, me miras mal, me atacas mi
> hablar
> mientras comes mcdonalds en discotecas
> americanas . . .
> . . . así que, por favor, no me
> hagas sufrir, sabes.

In "spanish" he perceives of himself as a "humble son of ESPAÑOL, one of my lenguas."

Tato Laviera is secure in a complex, contemporary manner. He writes convincingly and with a vast background of oral literature, in English, Spanish, Spanglish and in intralingual techniques mixing the languages. Not only is he quite aware of his Afro-Caribbean traditions, both on a folk level—in music, dance and mythology—and within a literary frame of reference, as in "cuban," "jamaican," "chorna," but he also celebrates all of these elements out of New York, amalgamating them into a whole.

Tato Laviera is so perfectly aware of traditional Puerto Rican values that he skillfully has his *persona*, an "abuelito," hand them out like lean, timeless aphorisms. No commentary is furnished or needed, no room for doubts allowed. This lack of commentary, of didactic explanatory writing, is one of Laviera's strong points. It is a technique that expects intelligent, attentive listeners and readers. This poet represents aspects both of the island world and the mainland. He is a very distinct New World phenomenon and in many ways a new species, a New Man. In "grafiteros," he links with ease mythical dimensions of Taíno stone etchings with potential postnuclear New York subway graffiti. The Lower East Side, which we know from his "Loisaida Street: Latinas Sing" section of *La Carreta*, is present in his "criollo story," the account of a tremendous *borrachera*.

Tato Laviera has to be credited also for being an astute chronicler of street life, of street talk. His unfailing ear for nuances, for double talk, verbal facades and revelations, rhythms and sound in *chismes*, conversations, monologues, becomes evident in a series of unforgettable portraits, as in "brava," "enchul," "pana," and "pai." With his though "esquina dude," we get a chilling piece of dialectic barrio survival philosophy:

> . . . stubborness must cover all my
> angles, bro, y te lo digo sincerely,
> . . . i tell you that life is based
> on the moment, el momento, bro, that's
> destiny, to survive el momento that
> will decide death . . .
> . . .
> i'm glad you paid me, bro, porque,
> cuentas claras conservan amistades,
> you know esactly what i mean, gracias.

The telephone conversation in "m'ija" amounts to a superb, humorous exercise in feminine psychology, and in "boda" the reader is made witness to a delightful, rapidly delivered *bochinche*:

> . . . el tremendo chisme, which one of the two
> suegras will ride the limousine, la grande,
> con aire acondicionado, the best man is late,
> big lenguas are saying, "te lo dije que a
> ése no se puede trostear, se llevó el oro al
> ponchop para poner la plata a los anillos,
> . . .
> . . . y el papá,
> desembarcó un tremendo suspiro, dándole
> un beso al redentor, "gracias dios mío,
> que aguanté esta jodienda, y llevé a mi hija hasta
> el altar.
> ("boda".)

The inherent dramatic qualities in these poems will take no one by surprise who has seen their creator take the stage at the Nuyorican Poets' Café or taken note of Laviera the playwright. It is not by chance, then, that Teatro 4 and the Center for Puerto Rican Studies at Hunter College, New York, offered on March 24, 1984, an evening with "Am-e-Rican. Poemas teatralizados de Tato Laviera," with the author as actor and co-director.

Tato Laviera's humor, his quick grasp for it wherever he finds it, serves him well in many of his works. He brings lofty Greek mythology down to busy Greek restaurants in New York: he sees Greeks more like Puerto Ricans anyway ("greek"). In "praying," we have a hilarious, slightly absurdist satire of Puerto Rican religious fervor:

> . . . papá dios está prendío, los "puerto ricans"
> están "overloading the numerous requests,"
> . . .
> . . . them puerto rican
> ladies, they pray non-stop, when they pray, they
> pray for everybody else. . .

. . .
. . . but papá dios said, to please tell them
puerto ricans, that he'll listen to their every
desire, if they will give papá dios un brakecito,
concho, "y déjenme dormir, de vez en cuando,
duerman ustedes, por favor."

But this author is capable also of sharp irony and proves highly sensitive to arrogance, pretense or an imperialist mentality, as in "english":

our backbones
constantly
searching
for-your-greatness
that
will re-define
ambitions
in-your-language

His "dictador" poem takes a clear anti-totalitarian stance and cuts through seemingly benevolent rhetoric to reveal the speaker's camouflaged cynical self-interest. In the work pertaining to political and party definitions, Laviera seizes the "revolutionary" attitude concisely:

it
 has
  to
   be
    resolved
     through
     blood
      . . .
       love
        knows
         no
          compromise

He recognizes the Populares' dilemma:

limbo
limping in circles,
still buying time,
the indecision of goals,
("popular")

Yet he shows himself conciliatory towards Muñoz Marín when he evokes that man's youth in the Lower East Side and the historical moment of the nascent Commonwealth status, ("don luis muñoz marín"). The stout defender of statehood, Ferré, fares worse with the writer:

instead of statehood senator of u.s.a.,
why not governor of an independent state,
of a puerto rican-japanese state,

. . .

protecting the interests of the u.s.a.

. . .

plenty of money and military bases,
and a faithful ally to the western world."
("don luis a. ferré")

Clear-cut and sharp as a razor blade is the message of another political option, represented by Juan Mari Bras and the PSP in a visual poem:

. . .
la
in
de
pen
den
cia
no
se
com
pra
. . .
("mari bras")

Tato Laviera is a bilingual poet of the people, for the people a poet of selfhood, sensuousness and life, of critical sanity, humaneness, warmth and triumphant joy. Above all, he is a poet of love and respect. I believe, he has once again brought out the essence of his own multi-faceted people in "boricua":

> we are a people
> who love to love
> we are loving
> lovers who love
> to love respect.

In the fragmented, menaced world we all live in, poetic voices like Tato Laviera's will be needed for a long time to come.

Wolfgang Binder
University of Erlangen
Federal Republic of Germany

Ethnic Tributes

book   (to all poets, all of us)

the day arrived,
published book date,
calling mamá to
collect blessings
roots, inside
nicolás kanellos
writing room,
he opens a spanish
literature bookcase . . .
the smell of all that
history, the moistured
aging scent of relics:
the bible, cervantes,
shakespeare, jefferson,
lope de vega, brecht,
unamuno, nietzche,
neruda, hemingway,
pietri, toast to
him, greeting him
giving him
sacred space, and now,
feast: the mexican
singer marco antonio
muñiz, honors him
with puerto rican
composer rafael hernández'
morning medley melodies . . . . .
meditating, the book
caught itself in the
macho of the "urbane,"
the virgin first copy,
just touched the author's
nervously expressive
trembling hands and,
looking from the inner
sanctum of his eyes,

he opened me, fingers
gently upon my covers,
. . . sanctifying
feeling of accomplishment
beatified my total self,
and, in a quiet breath of
aspiration, i looked upon
the him and the her reflections,
found on the first page
of a new book and i
allowed myself to call me
beautiful

intellectual

so historically total
so minutely precise
so accurately detailed
so politically active
so grammatically arrogant
so academically prepared
so literally perfect
so ethnically snobbish
so aristocratically professional
so if you want to challenge me,
be prepared to lose the argument,
for i am too humanly infallible
about my researched assertions,
so take it or leave it,
the latter is your wisest choice,
do not arouse my anger,
i will reduce you to a
bibliographical ibidem,
demoting you to childhood,
in other words,
come out to kill,
and be dead
from the start.

boricua

we are a people
who love to love
we are loving
lovers who love
to love respect,
the best intentions
of friendship,
and we judge from
the moment on, no
matter who you are,
and, if we find
sincere smiles,
we can be friends,
and, if we have a
drink together,
we can be brothers,
on the spot, no
matter who you are,
and we have a lot
of black & white
& yellow & red
people whom we
befriend, we're
ready to love
with you, that's
why we
say, let there
be no prejudice,
on race, color is
generally color-blind
with us, that's our
contribution, all
the colors are tied
to our one,
but we must fight
the bad intentions,

we must respect
each other's values,
but guess what,
we're not the only ones,
and we offer what your
love has taught us,
and what you're worth
in our self-respect,
we are a people
who love to love
who are loving
lovers who love
to love respect.

arab

allah be praised
allah almighty
allah allah
allah be praised
protect us
allah the highest
all-knowing
all-merciful
all-faithful
allah, you come to us,
allah be praised, we will protect your laws,
allah be praised, we will protect your lands,
allah be praised, we will protect your name,
allah be praised, we will protect your name,
allah, we will protect ourselves,
allah, we will protect ourselves,
allah, we will protect your name,
allah, our hands are in your will,
allah, your will, allah, we're blinded,
    your will, allah, our will,
        allah, my will,
        allah, i will fight,
        allah, until we win,
        allah, until we win,
        allah, we win we win,
           we win we win,
             win we win,
              we win,
                in
             aaaaaaaaaaaaaaaaa
             llaaaaaaaaaaaaaah
             victory,
             your
             name!

black

full moonlight in central park
metropolitan house: la boheme
a soprano voice reaching
thirty thousand people sitting in
summer evening, the trumpets
sang, their winds circulating,
integrating and, there were
blacks who had suffered,
blacks who had been slaves,
blacks who were now chanting
to protect world interests,
african, caribbean, urban european,
black madame, a la leontyne price,
cabling the world into classical
aesthetic leadership,
its humanity,
its humanity,
a testament
to all who
over
come
song,
song,
song!

chinese

all
those
fa
ces
hap
py
el
ders
trea
ted
with
res
pect
by
the
clan
won
der
ful
chi
nese
cul
ture
all
pay
ing
hom
age
to
the
wise

cuban
for Nicolás Guillén

base prieta jerigonza
(escondida en lo cristiano)
huracán secreto
luna llena se desvela
se desborda:

> ¡bajó el cielo, maraña gloriosa!
> ¡bajó el cielo, espíritu espanto!
> ¡bajó el cielo, guaguancó de mambo!
> ¡estrellas en coro, salen nicollenando!

base prieta jerigonza
(escondida en lo cristiano)
huracán secreto
luna llena se desvela
se desborda, sale OCHA
camino real, voz maravillosa:

> lo que vale es lo que vive en la conciencia,
> el que sabe de igualdad en su todo lo comenta,
> no hay quien embabuque al niche desengañado,
> en el secreto todo se guarda, todo se observa.

base prieta jerigoza
(escondida en lo cristiano)
huracán secreto
luna llena se revela
se desborda, se enamora:

> ¡se sabe que al dormir hay sueño
> prieto, ñañiguero, abacuado en ogunero
> changoteando madamas yorubistas
> adentro del sueño otro sueño
> yemayado de orishas
> sacudiendo caderas de europeo
> el origen se preserva
> al vaivén de ideas claras
> al vaivén de ideas claras
> ideas claras caribeñas!

salió el sol, sus rayos atravesando
     rayos, largas piernas afriqueñas
     rayos, trompetas charanga europea
     rayos, tambores indígenas se encuentran
     rayos, rompiendo todo esclavo
     rayos, preservando colores de resguardo
     rayos, con los viejos africanos
     libremente exclamando:

     ¡somos los mismos, los mismos éramos
     y, aún más, un nuevo cambio:
     no somos ni negros, no somos ni africanos
     somos humanos, respaldándonos, somos humanos
     así, que salga el sol, así que siga la luna
     así, que salga el sol, así que siga la luna
     así, que suba el cielo, adiós al sueño
     yo le canto a la lumbre del glorioso despertar
     yo le canto a la lumbre del glorioso despertar!

english

so
exquisite
general
overtones
tonalities
transfused
transcending
growing
definitions
expansions
most-advanced
researching
ex-creating-out
clearest
clarity
orgasms
of
confusion
we-hate-love
your
forced
indulgences
our
backbones
constantly
searching
for-your-greatness
that
will
re-define
ambitions
in-your-language
we
struggle
to
make

everyone
humanistically
proud
of
your
relationship
to
the
growth
of
the
world

greek

looking to find modern mythology
in the descendents
of ancient playwrights, to see if
something rubbed off, was aristotle
brown in color, no, it couldn't be,
well, anyway, the new poets of god,
are making money, simply because the
poets were kept unemployed by some sleazy
characters throughout history,

where else could i find such
mythological realities, i wonder
if the greek scientists, who are
now board chairmen, were lighter in
skin than the playwrights, that
might explain the reason for their poets'
expulsion, no, it couldn't be . . .

well, anyway, i love all greeks,
and all the colors they may wish
to add to this poem, but i always
think they are puerto ricans,
that's why i only mythologize
in greek restaurants open
twenty-four hours a day
in new york.

irish
(odes)

march song

bobby	sands	irish	land
sands	irish	land	bobby
irish	land	bobby	sand
land	bobby	sands	irish
bobby	sands	irish	land

eulogy

warriors never die
never smile warriors
never smile never die
hear the cry
hear the cry
hear the cry
warriors never cry
smile warriors never
smile cry warriors
always smile cry
warriors always smile
cry always never cry
hear the cry smile
hear the smile cry
always always
hear the cry
patriotic smile

spirit

as i die i live
the earth purity
body without water
bread i cleansed
i bathed in irish
green fragrance
freely flowing
forever flag
fasting

freedom
fasting
ireland
ira-land
free ireland
free ireland
my gut of dignity
of trust of truth
of love i gave all
i gave all
to free ireland
to free ireland

italian
(ballad)

young dude
is old dude
is same dude
we grew dude

young dude
is old dude
is same dude
we grew dude

he sang blues
the old blues
the new blues

the top blues
youngsters were
old dudes old dudes
were young dudes

the lyrics distinguished
all decades agreed with
the crooner the loner
the proud style
the voice range
transcended
his lifetime

so always always sing
like blue eyes
young blue eyes
old blue eyes

same blue eyes
so always always sing
please, blue eyes.

jamaican

reach their guts into the caribbean
the second africa, divided by yemaya
reach their guts into the third world
marley-manley emerging people
reach their guts into urban america
reggae-reggae, modern english
reach their guts into ethiopia
rastafarian celebrated deities
reach their guts into washington square park
jamaican english, folkloric blackness
reach their guts into puerto ricans
where we shared everything for free
yeah, brother, very good, very, very
good, yeah, real good!

japanese
(joke?)

> he was ten years old in 1942
> when they killed mama-san
> and papa-san (street vendors
> in pearl harbor) the day on
> the japanese attack, on
> december 7th, he fled to
> the mountains of a deserted
> hawaiian island, way up there
> near a volcano, he grew to
> find peace, the fifties, the
> sixties, the seventies, the
> volcano was erupting, he came
> down from the mountains when
> he was fifty years old in 1982
> he arrived at sea-level
> he was prepared to die
> and, guess what, he saw
> the billboard toyota ads
> and he thought the japanese
> had won the war.

jewish

we stand the pain of time
we stand across the pain of time
we withstood the harshest pain of time
we know you know that:
we will never again be persecuted
we will never again be lynched
we will protect ourselves from the world
yiddish always! we have a lot of names
in many languages we will communicate
yiddish always! we have a lot of names
in many languages we will communicate
the elders all taught the second tongue
we might be spanish, french, german, americans
yiddish always, we all can speak one tongue
we have a lot of names, in many languages
we stand the pain of time
we stand across the pain of time
we withstood all the pain of time
and we live, side by side, in peaceful harmony
but never, never, again.

russian

she scraped the church floor
with fervent devotion she shined marble
climbing up to the lord's resurrection
looking down, the madonna selected
her altar boys and choir boys who
walked her home into her apartment
she seduced young virgins
she painted her own saintly cherubims
twelve and thirteen years old
playing with her slowly and fruitfully
the first time, but she wanted
the second time, right away, and
the young boys were overtaken by her
brutal strength passion so strong
that the seraphims collapsed out of
sheer exhaustion, and then
she devoured them totally
she taught them to be macho
she taught them to be men
she polished fourteen carat chalices.

spanish

your language outlives your world power.
but the english could not force you to change
the folkloric flavorings of all your former colonies
makes your language a major north and south american
tongue.
the atoms could not eradicate your pride,
it was not your armada stubborness
that ultimately preserved your language.
it was the nativeness of the spanish,
mixing with the indians and the blacks,
who joined hands together, to maintain your precious
tongue,
just like the arabs, who visited you for
eight hundred years, leaving the black
skin flowers of andalucía,
the flamenco still making beauty with your tongue.
it was the stubborness of the elders,
refusing the gnp national economic language,
not learning english at the expense of
much poverty and suffering, yet we maintained
your presence, without your maternal support.
Spain, you must speak on behalf of your language,
we await your affirmation of what we have fought
to preserve.
ESPAÑOL, one of my lenguas, part of my tongue,
I'm gonna fight for you, i love you, spanish,
i'm your humble son.

¡ahí viene, ahí viene!
no me queda más remedio,
vivo adentro de la primera milla,
entonces yo la voy a esperar
corriendo desesperado hacia
el centro de wall street
esperando a la prostituta
madamo del maldito TEN
que evaporizará mis espíritus,
reduciéndome a una teoría
matemática adentro del NINE
por los cincuenta canales
nervios electrónicos del EIGHT
se penetran los aparatos ovarios
del satélite capitalizando el SEVEN
en la computadora musical del SIX
QUE ME LLEVA DESESPERADO
hacia un rumbo sin destino
que me convierte iluminosamente
en un brujo amante del impacto FIVE
¡ahí viene, ahí viene!
yo, cerrando los ojos,
yo, rogando a lo indígena,
que me separe del miedo,
que salve a todos los niños del FOUR
corriendo desesperado hacia
el centro de wall street
esperando a la prostituta
madamo del maldito THREE
que me hundirá en la tierra,
la que dio a luz a los neutrones del TWO
la que quemará mi existencia con un vapor,
fuego, caliente, destructor, fuego,
metiéndose en las raíces naturales del ONE.
¡aquí viene, aquí viene!
el impacto que bombardeará

nuestras almas explotando las caderas del desarrollo,
ZERO
la tierra despidiéndose de la luna
besándola con un cantito de la NADA.
hacia el rumbo sin destino,
hacia el rumbo sin destino,
quién sabe lo que se puede hacer
para evitar el maldito compás
de esa bomba en plena nuclear,
de esa bomba en plena nuclear.

VALUES

café

dry
roasted
out
of
sun
café
crushed
café
grinded
boiled
"colao"
café
aroma
into
nostrils
fresh
caffeine
drugging
sleep
into
an
awake
café
smells
deep
breath
long
stretch
eyes
open
café
day
light
mmmm
café
sabor

boyhood

behind our puerto rican santurce
house on bella vista street
buried in the yard we found a coffin
jorgito and i kept the secret
for two weeks we gathered enough
courage sunday after dinner
we dug for it
we paced around it
we opened it with a car jack
we found a black and white
nationalist flag
we looked at each other
"let's unveil it,"
"yeah, let's go all the way,"
we uncovered the flag
we found an arsenal of
weapons underground
live ammunition
patria o muerte slogans
land or death
there was no other choice
we looked at each other
we closed the coffin
we buried it with soil
we kept the secret.

negrito

el negrito
vino a nueva york
vio milagros
en sus ojos
su tía le pidió
un abrazo y le dijo,
"no te juntes con
los prietos, negrito."
el negrito
se rascó los piojos
y le dijo,
"pero titi, pero titi,
los prietos son negritos."
su tía le agarró
la mano y le dijo,
"no te juntes con
los molletos, negrito".
el negrito
se miró sus manos
y le dijo,
"pero titi, pero titi,
así no es puerto rico."
su tía le pidió
un besito y le dijo,
"si los cocolos te molestan,
corres; si te agarran, baila.
hazme caso, hazme caso,
negrito."
el negrito
bajó la cabeza
nueva york lo saludó,
nueva york lo saludó,
y le dijo,
"confusión"
nueva york lo saludó
y le dijo,
"confusión."

abuelito

cuando
el
padre
regaña
al
hijo
el
hijo
baja
la
cabeza
y
no
se
atreve
a
responder.
lo
máximo
es
el
orgullo
y
el
respeto
de
ser
hombre.
la
mentira
es
el
ogro
del
opio.
siempre

se
pide
permiso
al
pasar
entre
dos
personas.
a
los
mayores
de
familia
se
les
pide
la
bendición.

jíbaro

end of spring harvest,
el jíbaro mathematically
working the sun's energies,
nurturing every fruit to
blossom perfectly,
singing about
earth, la tierra,
time after time, acre after acre,
year after year, the land provided.
end of spring harvest,
el jíbaro's guitar
on la carreta,
pulling, ploughing slowly
towards sunset,
towards la cena,
towards the afternoon breeze,
land, love, moon,
the lyrics emerged,
décimas in place,
the ever-present "lo le lo lai,"
and then, the song,
canción.

ay bendito

oh, oh. ¡ay virgen!
fíjese, oiga, fíjese.
ay, bendito.
pero, ¿qué se puede hacer?
nada, ¿verdad?
ave maría.
ah, sí. ah, sí, es así.
pues, oiga,
si es la verdad.
pero, ¿qué se puede hacer?
nada, ¿verdad?
fíjese, oiga, fíjese.
mire, mire.
oh, sí, ¡hombre!
oiga, así somos
tan buenos, ¿verdad?
bendito.
¡ay, madre!
¡ay, dios mío!
¡ay, dios santo!
¡me da una pena!
ay, si la vida es así, oiga.
pero, ¿qué se puede hacer?
nada, ¿verdad?
fíjese, oiga, fíjese.
oiga, fíjese.

de pueblo

todos somos puertorriqueños, olvídate,
hasta el fin; pero, si
los gallitos de manatí
se enfrentan con
los cangrejeros de santurce,
no se sorprendan si
los cangrejeros le cortan
el cuello a un gallo
al comienzo del juego profesional
y no se sorprendan si
los gallitos le mentan a
la madre o a la abuela del
primer cangrejo prieto
y no se sorprendan si
todos bebemos juntos
emborrachando las
carcajadas.

deporte

métele mano mátalo brother
con un bolo punch derecha
larga al costado empínale
los puños con un fuerte
izquierdazo left jab al hocico
de sus ojos apabúllalo con
cuatro uppercuts durísimos
está sentido no oigas la campana
no le des break dale al pómulo
derecha puñal en la espina
dorsal de su corazón apúntale
combinaciones right-left
gancho de izquierda manufacturado
en la tierra dale la paliza
del siglo con los codos aterrizando
en las mejillas para que se le
caigan los dientes del impacto
de un over right machete para
que le partas el puente de
la nariz en dos destrúyele
el cuerpo hasta que se le caigan
las manos y cuando él no pueda
más cuando esté ya agotado
de descarga tan grande échate
hacia atrás y castígalo con
un martillazo en plena boca
y déjalo muerto sin que el
oficial tenga que contar a diez.

pai

compa primo cabo
compa primo cabo
socio venga acá
no se vaya disgustao
le doy la plena razón
por sus acciones
recuérdese que usted
es el padre de su hija
tiene razón en defenderla
no se apure compa
lo hizo bien
el buen ejemplo empieza
con el pai
y yo le digo
que cuando usted se paró
a llamarle la atención
al canalla que humilló
a su hija y cuando él
le contestó estrujadamente
y cuando usted le metió
tremenda pescozá ya yo
tenía las manos en mis
bolsillos y lo que iba
a salir era el cañon
que usaron los guerrilleros
para ganar la guerra de
vietnam y estaba calientito
así que usted siempre
tranquilo y yo le aseguraré
su espalda porque usted
sabe que es mi compa, pai.

three-way warning poem
(for José Luis González)

1.	*sin nombre*	2.	*sin nombre the first*
	en		ste
	el		reo
	fon		type
	do		pu
	del		er
	nu		to
	yo		rri
	ri		que
	can		ño
	hay		sí
	un		yes
	pu		we
	er		can
	to		cut
	rri		you
	que		all
	ño		in

pana

i was in jail, brother. jail, brother.
encarcelao, under, bro, allá adentro,
solo, alone, bro, all by myself,
even with another name; y ese tipo
that i barely knew long ago,
he claimed he and my brother
had changed my diapers and
that he had seen me grow up,
desde chiquito, bro, he made me laugh,
he knew my case was a bum rap,
he knew i could defend my black belt,
but i was from his neighborhood,
it was his duty, he felt, to protect,
and that night he became the malote,
he went cell by cell setting the law
that he would cut heads with his teeth,
as machete, if any harm came my way,
i was released, he was doing life,
i go see him once a month, religiously,
bro, i slide him some good jades,
and i don't care if i get caught,
you know why, bro, porque
ese tipo es mi pana.

.

graffiters

in the near
distant future
archaeologists
will find ancient
hieroglyphics
fossils under
ground on subway
steel columns
inside the tunnel
underneath east
river they found
artifacts resembling
modern taíno symbols
the archaelogists
analyzed signatures
interpreted to read
"our imprint to the
future we graffiters
wanted to somehow
survive the nuclear
holocaust to be
remembered for
whatever else
emerged."

grafiteros

los oídos enchufados con cassettes estereofónicos
caminando como guerrilleros allá abajo haciendo
música silenciosa con la firma presidencial del
progreso adentro de las raíces eléctricas ellos
escriben las señales bilingües odiadas como basura
como vandalismo los muchachitos del bronx y de
cualquier bloque hispano se sientan en los stoops
a diseñar los planes militares para penetrarse en
los sistemas alcantarillados para entrar a las
venas del subway a imprimir como fósiles la civi-
lización que será descubierta en el futuro incierto
ellos saben cómo preservar sus firmas nos estudian
científicamente el imprimatur de querer pertenecer
la ansiedad de acertar presencia con anuncios
modernos para inmortalizarse los muchachitos de
brooklyn y de cualquier bloque hispano guerrilleros
del silencio velando el horario de los trenes
cuándo vienen cuándo regresan mientras terminan
sus murales allá adentro en el hierro estancado
para asegurarse de un puesto microscópico en otras
generaciones hasta se ponen caretas de mono dándole
el gran susto al conductor.

nuyorican

yo peleo por ti, puerto rico,   ¿sabes?
yo me defiendo por tu nombre, ¿sabes?
entro a tu isla, me siento extraño, ¿sabes?
entro a buscar más y más,   ¿sabes?
     pero tú con tus calumnias,
     me niegas tu sonrisa,
     me siento mal, agallao,
     yo soy tu hijo,
     de una migración,
     pecado forzado,
     me mandaste a nacer nativo en otras tierras,
     por qué, porque éramos pobres, ¿verdad?
porque tu querías vaciarte de tu gente pobre,
ahora regreso, con un corazón boricua, y tú,
me desprecias, me miras mal, me atacas mi hablar,
mientras comes mcdonalds en discotecas americanas,
y no pude bailar la salsa en san juan, la que yo
bailo en mis barrios llenos de todas tus costumbres,
así que, si tú no me quieres, pues yo tengo
un puerto rico sabrosísimo en qué buscar refugio
en nueva york, y en muchos otros callejones
que honran tu presencia, preservando todos
tus valores, así que, por favor, no me
hagas sufrir, ¿sabes?

asimilao

assimilated? qué assimilated,
brother, yo soy asimilao,
así mi la o sí es verdad
tengo un lado asimilao.
you see, they went deep . . . . Ass
oh . . . . they went deeper . . . SEE
oh, oh, . . . they went deeper . . . ME
but the sound LAO was too black
for LATED, LAO could not be
trans*lated*, assimilated,
no, asimilao, melao,
it became a black
spanish word but
we do have asimilados
perfumados and by the
last count even they
were becoming asimilao
how can it be analyzed
as american? así que se
chavaron
trataron
pero no
pudieron
con el AO
de la palabra
principal, dénles gracias a los prietos
que cambiaron asimilado al popular asimilao.

criollo story

i was drunk, sunday morning
sitting at tompkins square park
i was drummed-all-night
hitting them cueros
while the people sang the coros
bomba, plena, guaguancó, even
boogie jazz baritone
and black-man-mean tyrone
brother-friend from the neighborhood
tyrone, the singing, the dancing
the mixing up with rum into vodka
lo que venga, bro, échalo pa' cá
tonight is to vacilar
jamaican liquors washed in
constant beers, imported
exported and of course
colt 45's pistoling into
the final killer, dry red
wine from some crazy punk
rocker brother i tell you that
i was drunk, farts galore
pigeons fled new york
the lower east side was on
civil alert, to tell you the
truth, i was dead drunk, brother-man
tyrone telling me, "brother,
you look so bad, that if you
were thunderbird wine, i would
not even drink a free sample."
i was so drunk i could not even laugh
and then salvation time
"for you, mira, mondongo"
i thought tyrone was goofing on me
"you look like a mondongo yourself"
"no, no, not you, mira, i mean, HUMERA,
for HUMERA, mondongo, bro, adela,

she opens at five o'clock, let's
eat some of that tripe."

we walked into adela's five-
thirty morning mountain smell
of madrugada simmering concrete
puerto rican new york radio JIT
cuatro-music, recordando a borinquen
songs made famous by don santiago
grevi, and the crushed plantains
bollitos rounded boricua matzo all
around cleaned vinagrette tripe
and patitas de cerdo pig feet,
softened to a melted overblown
delicacy, brother, and i tell you that
down went the russian vodka
the alcohol disappeared with
bites of calabaza-pumpkin pieces
and the one hundred proof bacardí
was choked by un canto de yautía
tubers that were rooting the european
dry red wine into total decolonization
and the broth, brother, EL CALDO
condimented garlic onions
peppered with whole tomatoes
that were melted by the low
heat, ese caldo was woefully
seducing the jamaican liquors
into compatibility, and down
went the BORRACHERA, bro, and
without talking, i looked
across to tyrone's second
plate, i thanked my brother
with a smile, as we kissed
adela, and what the hell
we took the number six into
orchard beach, on section
three, and we blew the sun
as we had serenaded the moon.

craqueao

four and one half billion
years old we are i heard
we are the most advanced
human beings believe me
i read that they study us
in chemistry we come from
organic soup dna and dinosaurs
who died and then the flowers
gave air i don't know all
the details but brother
we came from the sea and
we adapted to the air
we were fish
éramos pescao bacalao
pregúntaselo a darwin
salimos del agua somos
familia de los reptiles y
las tortugas que no regresaron
al mar y después cuando
estábamos en tierra nosotros
éramos gorilas y monos yo
vine del chimpancé brother
entonces empezamos a hablar . . .
"óyeme, y ¿dónde está el darwin ese?"
"darwin está muerto."
"¡seguro, y tú craqueao!"

esquina dude

i like and dislike, like the good
dislikes the bad in everything, bro
nothing is better than nothing, bro
i integrate what i like, i reject
what i don't like, bro, nothing of
the past that is present is sacred
everything changes, bro, anything
that remains the same is doomed to
die, stubborness must cover all my
angles, bro, y te lo digo sincerely
my judgement, bro, mi juicio, bro, bro
bro, i tell you that life is based
on the moment, el momento will
catch up to you, bro, i always prepare
myself for the constant ever present
moment, bro, the past, the present, the
future has nothing to do with the moment, and
yes, there are times when i open my blade
to cut, bro, i hope you understand
sincerely, sinceramente, bro, that if i
wound you, you probably deserved it
but i'll take you to the hospital if
you're still alive, and i'll face the
charges, but if we face each other, bro
de cara a cara, from face to face
you will know that you deserved that moment
porque, everybody knows i don't cut
unless you were meant to be cut, bro
so, be careful what you learn from me
and be careful not to use it against me
i love you, tú sabes that i do, de corazón
bro, but i might have to kill you
bro, but i hope you survive to be
my enemy or my friend, i'll take

you alive, either way, that's the way i
think, bro, that's my ideology
you better respect it bro, chévere
right on, hey, you're cold, bro
don't worry, i will kiss you openly
on the baseball field, nobody will
mess with you, i know you understood
everything i said, i know you don't
need a bilingual dictionary, what i said
can cut into any language, this is about
your life, i know you play no games
i'm glad you paid me, bro, porque
cuentas claras conservan amistades
you know exactly what i mean, gracias.

coqueta

sa
bes
e
res
be
lla

con
tes
tas

"si
gue

mi
ran
do

sue
ños."

enchulá

unfortunately, my new loves are
short range, i tried many times
to be long range, pero, time and
time again, you know, me decepcionaban
ahora, acepto los amores short range
honey, y te digo que mis amores se
ponen celosos, qué vaina, yo ahora
liberándome, queriendo short range
y ahora, todos ellos me quieren, y qué
long range, te lo digo, cuando yo era
buena, tú sabes, lo que yo quiero decir
entonces, me trataban mal, qué chavienda
ahora no soy tan buena, y los tengo
controlao, los hombres son masoquistas
verdad, te lo juro, me siento liberada
pero, concho, el diablo aquel todavía
me tiene la vida enchulá.

m'ija

i've been dying to call you m'ija
to tell you that last night i was
celebrating nothing, nothing to do
no money, no dress, nobody, m'ija,
un tremendo down, life is hard, even
on my birthday, eso te ha pasao a ti
también, verdad, but then, it all
changed, mamá called, she cooked a
"comidita," and she sewed a "nueva
blusita," real nice, and she baked
my favorite "postre," and one of my
"padrinos" remembered and there
was an envelope waiting and of course
i could have called him, m'ija, and
he would have been kneeling at my
door, but my pride insisted on my
pride, anyway, my family had remembered
yo estaba "llenita" and mamá gave me a
big abrazo after i blew out the candles
and i said to myself, "the hell with
it," i'm gonna get me a sexy dress
even if i bite my nails tomorrow for
falling behind on all my payments
pero, m'ija, i bought a sexy dress
and i went to the corso knowing he
would find me there, but i was going
to boogie and dance so freely that
i saw the tension in his jealous eyes
and he came to me to disculparse
and i really wanted him, anyway, so
muchas luces y boleros y besitos
y besos, del resto, mi amiga, ya tú
sabes, nena, lo celebré bien chévere
bien, bien chévere, te lo puedo contar
a ti todo, para eso somos amigas.

brava

they kept on telling me
"tú eres disparatera"
they kept on telling me
"no se entiende"
they kept on telling me
"habla claro, speak spanish"
they kept on telling me
telling me, telling me
and so, the inevitable
my spanish arrived
"tú quieres que yo hable
en español" y le dije
all the spanish words
in the vocabulary, you
know which ones, las que
cortan, and then i proceded
to bilingualize it, i know
yo sé that que you know
tú sabes que yo soy that
i am puertorriqueña in
english and there's nothing
you can do but to accept
it como yo soy sabrosa
proud ask any streetcorner
where pride is what you defend
go ahead, ask me, on any street-
corner that i am not puertorriqueña,
come dímelo aquí en mi cara
offend me, atrévete, a menos
que tú quieras que yo te meta
un tremendo bochinche de soplamoco
pezcozá that's gonna hurt you
in either language, así que
no me jodas mucho, y si me jodes
keep it to yourself, a menos
que te quieras arriesgar

y encuentres and you find
pues, que el cementerio
está lleno de desgracias
prematuras, ¿estás claro?
are you clear? the cemetery
is full of premature short-
comings.

boda

the boda gathering modeling a wide display
of mademoiselle bazaar's modern rentals
on a bright june saturday afternoon of
bochinches, money problems, late musicians
el fotógrafo getting non-contract requests
y el tremendo chisme, which one of the two
suegras will ride the limousine, la grande
con aire acondicionado, the best man is late
big lenguas are saying, "te lo dije que a
ése no se puede trostear, se llevó el oro al
ponchop para ponerle plata a los anillos"
la novia es presbiteriana, but the groom's
mother is a big shot in her catholic parish
and she's forcing a second ceremony, one of
the smallest damas está "prendía," her dress
is too long, and she was placed last in line
she swore to count nine fingers from this day
on, one for each month, to see if la novia
"había metido las patas," the gathering outside the
church "encontraron los trajes
bien lindos," but el borrachón commented that
"the tuxedos esos son cosas pa' los prietos"
the friend of one of the caballeros embarrassed
him as the caballero was kissing the hand of
the dama "del traje colorao," by saying
"take the tuxedo off, you have to return it
tomorrow," the boy friend of another dama
caught her flirting with another caballero
the boy friend came over, there were tensions
at the end of the line, the women with rollers
for la fiesta later clicked their cameras
wanting to be novias again, the processional
music began, the best man llegó, la novia
towards the altar marched, they reached the
two reverends, el novio's hand, a nervous
testament, the ceremony began y el papá

desembarcó un tremendo suspiro dándole
un beso al redentor, "gracias dios mío
que aguanté esta jodienda y llevé a mi hija hasta el
altar."

puertorriqueña

oh no te apures
yo te los saco
uno a uno
si es familia
lo que tú quieres
yo te lo doy
dos si tú te
quedas aquí conmigo
tres y cuatro
yo te los saco
cinco yo te daré
seis si tú te
quedas aquí conmigo
siete yo te daré
ocho si tú te
quedas aquí conmigo
pase lo que pase
oh no te apures
yo te los saco
siempre y cuando
lo
   tu
     yo
       sea
         to
           í
             to
               mío
                 'tá
                to'
                   bien
                    si
                     no
                       nin
                       gu
                        no

chorna

tembandumba, now an elder,
gracefully watched the time:

"tatarabuela" her son calling her
"tatarabuela" her grandson calling her
"tatarabuela" her great-grandson calling her
"tatarabuela" her great great grandson
           her fourth generation was born, calling her
           all of us calling her today "tátarabuela!"

tembandumba, now an elder,
gracefully watched the time:

she was a tatarabuela . . . . fourth generation
she was bisabuela . . . . third generation
she was abuela . . . . second generation
she was madre . . . . first generation
she had them in two lands
she had them in spanish
she had them in english
she had them black and white
she had them duplicated with beautiful women.

tembandumba, now an elder,
gracefully watched the time:

"tatarabuela" her great-great grandson-tataranieto
           turned sixteen, the generations called
           him macho-macho, bear children, macho.
           her great great great grandson-chorno,
           her fifth generation was born, calling her
           all of us calling her today "CHORNA!"

tembandumba, now an elder,
tembandumba, chorna, mulata construction
elegantly walking, shaking forever youthful,
time and time and time and time again!

thinking

muerte, el respirar suspira
muerte, careciendo lágrimas
muerte, tempestad infinita
muerte, tú tienes las llaves
muerte, tú tienes las llaves
del pensar que no conozco
por eso te espero
por eso te peleo
por eso te odio
muerte, tú tienes las llaves
y yo, como veo lo que siento
y yo, como siento lo que no veo
  yo, como siento lo que no veo
      como siento lo que no veo
        siento lo que no veo
          lo que no veo
            que no veo
              no veo
                veo
                  eo,
                    o o o u a e i o
                    siento
                    sonidos
                    así
                    que
                    vendré
                    regresaré
                    de nuevo
                    en
                    al
                    go

muerte, un perro
      se para
      me mira
      me mira
      lo siento

se va andando
y yo, sigo caminando, buscando la reencarnación

talking

te
lo
digo
bien
claro
tenemos
que
buscar
firmeza
tenemos
que
buscar
firmeza
firmeza
tenemos
que
trabajar
la
vida
pague
o
no
pague
y
después
de
la
firmeza
uno
puede
hasta
vacilar
por
largos
ratos.

praying

papá dios está agallao, ya no puede soportar
los "puerto ricans" están orando overtime
no dejamos dormir a dios, está volviéndose loco
con las comiquerías de nosotros, siempre chavándole
la vida, papá dios está prendío, los "puerto ricans"
están "overloading the circuits with numerous requests"
te lo juro, créemelo, yo te lo advertí, lo escribí,
papá dios está enfogonao, deme esto, consígame
aquello, dele luz a mi vida, la com puta dora
tiene corto circuito, las operadoras "complaining"
a la supervisora, "qué diablo' hablan esas viejas,
rezan el rosario, murmurando como hormigas, their
spanish is unintelligible, they pray too fast"
dios-te-salve-maría-llena-eres-de-padre-nuestro-
gloria-al-padre-y-a-las-galletitas-y-el-chocolate-
caliente-amén, we don't understand.

the angels brought a lawsuit to the supreme
court of heaven, protesting puerto rican prayers
"we cannot pick up their signals, them puerto rican
ladies, they pray non-stop, when they pray, they
pray for everybody, their prayers are over-
flowing their allotted time, and it's working
against you, papá dios, we cannot answer their
prayers, they must be wondering, 'how come papá
dios does not reply?' they are taking over
the english channels, we cannot identify the items,
judge strictly for yourself, look at this daily sample,
just those pentecostals alone are driving the holy
spirit insane, all they want is transformations,
transformations, we're not coming down on them
puerto rican bodies, those crazy people are praying
themselves into our jobs, all they want are crazy
indian angels to come down, to assist some crazy
spiritualist, and we don't understand those native
dialects, papá dios, please change the laws."

papá dios got up and said . . . "Bendito, they work so
hard, bendito, they are so passive, i never get
angry with my worthy faithful subjects, it is
just that some crazy puerto rican poet is misinforming
the people, i'm not enfogonao," papá dios ordered
a new computerized system to solve the inundation
problem, but papá dios said to please tell them
puerto ricans that he'll listen to their every
desire, if they will give papá dios un brakecito,
concho, "y déjenme dormir. De vez en cuando
duerman ustedes, por favor."

dancing

i'll go out dancing
in the heat of salsa
i'll go out dancing
the adventures of my choice
i'll go out dancing
casablanca-corso-ochentas
broadway ninety-six style
i'll go out dancing
silk and gold and high-tech
french alla italiana dressed
in latino modern dress
i'll go out dancing
moving it, feeling it
living it, holding it
live and disco music
i'll go out dancing
hips that swing, curves expanding
dancing, the coro is chanting
dancing, turns entangling
dancing, sonero attacking
dancing, percussion bombarding
dancing, brass reacting
dancing, steps are snapping
música, música, música, música
clave-clave, clap, clap, clap
dancing, dancing, dancing
i'll go out dancing
heads underneath the cymbals
hands gouging pianos
everything touching
dancing, bodies integrating
dancing, climaxing, sweating
dancing, dancing
the night is wild
no sense of time
i'll go out dancing

salsa society dancing
and i danced
dancing
totally
digging
giving
and
we danced
the night
away
we danced
the night
away.

POLITICS

political

i'm pushed, i'm being pushed, pushed,
i'm pushed, i'm being pushed, pushed,
into the gutter, i'm being pushed,
into boiling point anger,
i'm being pushed, pushed,
yet i retain control,
yet i lean back,
yet i turn the other cheek,
yet i look to god for patience,
i'm being pushed, pushed,
into violent verbal action,
that tells me something,
i must do something i must
contribute to my community,
i must get involved,
i'm pushed, i'm being pushed, pushed,
yet i take alternative roads,
to keep away from the involvement,
because community leadership,
leads to broken marriages,
leads to lack of trust,
you do and do for the people,
and the people will stab you
in the back, so, i do nothing,
but knock on cold steel
with a rubber hammer,
attempting to penetrate,
until my soul no longer sweats,
but then, one day, i heard
music on the other side of
steel and i wrote down the
lyrics, marching with every
beat, shooting bullets of words
i sang the tune with my friends,
malice and injustice pushed again
and i made a citizen's arrest.

commonwealth

no, not yet, no, not yet
i will not proclaim myself,
a total child of any land,
i'm still in the commonwealth
stage of my life, wondering
what to decide, what to conclude,
what to declare myself.

i'm still in the commonwealth
stage of my life, not knowing
which ideology to select.

i'm still in the commonwealth
stage of my life, all of us
caught in a web of suspension,
light years away from the indians'
peaceful enclaves.

i'm still in the commonwealth
stage of my life, observing
the many integrated experiences
we took everything
and became everybody else.

i'm still in the commonwealth
stage of my life, but there's
not enough hatred in our hearts
to kill each other or to draw
blood for too long. ours
is a mental search
carved through a mainstream of options
but yet, somewhere
in the commonwealth, we all yearn
to feel our strengths,
to show our ultimate,
to find common wealth among us,
to close our eyes,
to find the total silence, silencio, silence,
to find . . . . . not one thing that unites us,

even in silence we are still
in the commonwealth stage of our lives.
so let's touch hands, friends and foes,
and stay together to hear each other's
sounds just for one moment, let's stay
tucked together, and maybe then, less
options, maybe then, hope.

dictador

nosotros hemos controlado por muchos
siglos aquí, así que, no queremos
fuerzas militares, a menos
que se evolucionen con nuestros
intereses propios; y por eso, yo le
digo a nuestro pueblo que resista
a los comunistas; hay que apoyarme
a mí, yo negociaré, por mi derecho
propio, y les prometo que haré todo
lo posible, para que en mi presidencia
las únicas armas en este país sean
las que yo les compre a nuestros grandes
amigos democráticos de los estados
unidos; diariamente hablo con los más
altos niveles militares de los ameri-
canos, y ellos nos han garantizado la
paz; así que, no tienen nada que du-
dar, trabajen la tierra, no hablen,
ruéguenle mucho a dios, odien a todos
los políticos, no jueguen con armas,
porque el fuego es el padrino de los
cementerios, paguen sus impuestos
religiosamente y esperen que yo ter-
mine los planes preliminares para
desarrollar y después planificar,
y despues votar por el plebiscito,
si es que sí o no debemos de votar;
este proceso se coge mucho tiempo
pero yo les juro que el próximo
presidente de esta nación será elec-
to por el pueblo, esperen un anuncio
pronto, sigan su máximo respaldo a
mi gobierno, centralmente adquiriendo
una posición internacional, he terminado
un tour del french riviera y les habla-
ré mañana directamente de italia, se

despide su gran elocuente presidente
de esta gran nación, y ustedes el gran
pueblo de este gran país, en éste su
exclusivo canal satélite de televisión,
y éste su único programa, que dios
siempre bendiga nuestra bandera, todos
a dormir, es hora del curfew, apagaré
toda la electricidad, todos a rezar,
bien calladitos, buenas noches, este
discurso fue pregrabado, gracias.

revolutionary

it
is
no
myth
it
has
to
be
resolved
through
blood
to
eliminate
the
ogre
the
permanent
infection
the
cancer
must
be
killed
it's
historically
clear
to
us
who
wage
constant
war
against
oppression
death
to

all
  oppressors
   free
    all
      political
       prisoners
        humanity
        and
          world
           peace
            now
             stop
              the
                bomb
                love
                  knows
                   no
                      compromise

popular

limbo
limping in circles
still buying time
the indecision of goals
still buying time, the leftists
and the rightists, and the left
right of all parties always
recruiting your unbalanced
members, like the jehovas and the
pentecostals preying on catholic
members, tired of european non-
spanish preachers, but the elders
in the social clubs and
muñoz are still your strongest
allies, and you're saved by
the mathematical dominoes of
so many puerto rican indecisions
and so many speculations, but
your soul moves in listless
circles turning like the old
man carousel, turning like the
old man carousel.

don luis muñoz marín

the poet jorge brandon, a sacred father-testament,
praises your history, your expansion, your moving
us into the center of the modern nineteenth century,
where man is most advanced; as we left the motherland,
the adventure of your policies and, most imporant,
the elders always speak of Constitution Day, in which
our flag, la bandera, was raised officially for the
first time, that moment, the free associated state,
or in historical terms, the commonwealth, that day,
muñoz, the elders hold in divine respect, there is
patriot in your name, muñoz, they gave you an up-
lifting walk, in the trains of your people's hand,
and they buried you with full honors, muñoz.

now i find traces of your bohemian days in the lower east side,
where you cleansed yourself, where you devised the
visions of your plans, where sometimes you won now
at the expense of future, but they love you, muñoz,
in the social clubs, the dominoes, the "palito," for
that day, it was an honorable and intelligent compromise,
it gave us time, they said you only went half way,
but you did not sell all the way, and the puerto
rican flag was up flying, out of a quietly persistent
struggle throughout its history, somehow your
pragmatic element was a necessary step onward, the
elders taught me to respect you, but you were in the
best of companies, the poet, jorge brandon, is
willing to defend you in front of anybody, and
i tell you, muñoz, that's one man i listen to
right away, and i tell you, thank you, for buying
time, no matter what else is ever said, the elders
believe in you and i believe in the elders.

don luis a. ferré

there were no paintings
and no poems in his name,
the young artists painted albizu,
he started thinking of his grave,
don luis a. ferré fell asleep,
a vision came his way:

instead of state senator of the u.s.a.,
why not governor of an independent state,
of a puerto rican-japanese state,
methodologies and third world training,
protecting the interests of the u.s.a.,
teaching english and spanish,
to african and latin american states,
plenty of money and military bases,
and a faithful ally of the western world.

there were no paintings
and no poems in his name,
the young artists painted albizu,
he started thinking of his grave,
don luis a. ferré fell asleep,
a vision came his way:

why not the patriot ferré?
he could move the new progressive party,
to major cities of the u.s.a.,
and still be elected u.s. senator in florida
and eat crumbs two ways,
in puerto rico and in the u.s.a.

puerto rico, independence, yes,
estadistas still in power, yes,
all his enemies will pay tribute,
at least for that one day,
his memoirs will be published,
he will be quoted on the front page
of the n.y. times,
"it took me, the capitalist ferré,

to complete what the pragmatist muñoz
and the revolutionary albizu
had started long ago."
don luis a. ferré awoke,
he was highly perplexed,
one of his dreams had said, "yes."

socialista

no debe ser así, que ellos son prejuiciados
y excluidos, porque ellos expresan
su santa patriótica libertad, la búsqueda
de un más-abierto humanismo
y no se quejan de ser minoría, y hablan
claro, y son apabullados y acusados y ellos
siempre empujando, la contrariedad a los
beneficios de la ciudadanía se expresan los
teoréticos-pintores, folklore soberanía,
colores de país libre, rojo-poderoso-verde-fuerte
junto también al mar, desarrollándose todo,
el conjunto en las antillas se expresan
los que cantan el nuevo camino,
sus verdades se vuelven dicha en gran futureo
por las carreteras del paso-paso,
por las carreteras del paso-paso,
por las carreteras de dicha-dicha,
lo llevan al tronco, la montaña independencia,
la celebración era bien alta, bien hundida,
subiendo banderas, esperando las estrellas,
al compás sublime de la libertad, así que,
no debe ser así, que ellos sean menospreciados,
porque en cualquier corte, brother, a ellos
se les pueden entregar nuestras tierras, y en
cualquier cuadro se llenaría de las riquezas
más puras, pero al final, lo que
importaba era la tremenda responsabilidad
que llevaba la causa y la tremenda realización
que todavía nada se había perdido, y la tremenda
sensación de elogiar, tantos buenos compatriotas
del pasado, cuyos esfuerzos no fueron en
vano, y lo tremendísimo-más-grande, qué linda
es la bandera de puerto rico, flotando
sus quehaceres celestiales ruiseñoreándose con los
planetas al compás de su himno, declamado
por su pueblo, y su estrella, sola entre las estrellas.

mari bras

la
in
de
pen
den
cia
no
se
com
pra
no
se
com
pro
me
te
se
a
ga
rra
des
de
las
ra
í
ces

licenciado don pedro albizu campos

like the year eighteen ninety-eight
   a definitely pure-white-clear poem:
   "tierra, tierra, desamparada . . ."

like the year nineteen ninety-eight,
   a patriot when he lived,
   a patriot when he died
   became a definitely
   pure-white-clear poem:
     "tierra, tierra, aislada,
     "tierra, tierra, despreciada . . . "

like all the time you talked
to us, principled, as the
desperate one who pulls switch-
blades protecting turf,
   a hero whose grave is san juan's
   capitolio overlooking la perla
   sanctified by a definitely
   pure-white-clear poem:
     "tierra, tierra, eres mía,
     manoseada mía, despreciada
     mía, mía, yo te daré pecho."

you who never smiled,
we see your face, fighting
all attacks, everybody
loves you, condemns you
you conservative radical
of the nineteenth century,
your nationalism drove
deep down into our future,
   a delicate man revered in the streets,
   don pedro is don pedro is don pedro
   pedro and again he will ever live,
   as long as we're alive we praise a
   definitely pure-white-clear poem.
   such is the testament of his:

"borinquen, tierra mía,
divina, celosa, No Estado,
humana nación."
and proud like a definitely
pure-white-clear poem,
don pedro albizu campos,
forever imbedded in our souls.

AmeRícan

we gave birth to a new generation,
AmeRícan, broader than lost gold
never touched, hidden inside the
puerto rican mountains.

we gave birth to a new generation,
AmeRícan, it includes everything
imaginable you-name-it-we-got-it
society.

we gave birth to a new generation,
AmeRícan salutes all folklores,
european, indian, black, spanish,
and anything else compatible:

AmeRícan,   singing to composer pedro flores' palm
             trees high up in the universal sky!

AmeRícan,   sweet soft spanish danzas gypsies
             moving lyrics la española cascabelling
             presence always singing at our side!

AmeRícan,   beating jíbaro modern troubadours
             crying guitars romantic continental
             bolero love songs!

AmeRícan,   across forth and across back
             back across and forth back
             forth across and back and forth
             our trips are walking bridges!

             it all dissolved into itself, the attempt
             was truly made, the attempt was truly
             absorbed, digested, we spit out
             the poison, we spit out the malice,
             we stand, affirmative in action,
             to reproduce a broader answer to the
             marginality that gobbled us up abruptly!

AmeRícan,   walking plena-rhythms in new york,
             strutting beautifully alert, alive,
             many turning eyes wondering,

admiring!

AmeRícan,   defining myself my own way any way many
ways Am e Rícan, with the big R and the
accent on the í!

AmeRícan,   like the soul gliding talk of gospel
boogie music!

AmeRícan,   speaking new words in spanglish tenements,
fast tongue moving street corner "que
corta" talk being invented at the insistence
of a smile!

AmeRícan,   aboundng inside so many ethnic english
people, and out of humanity, we blend
and mix all that is good!

AmeRícan,   integrating in new york and defining our
own destino, our own way of life,

AmeRícan,   defining the new america, humane america,
admired america, loved america, harmonious
america, the world in peace, our energies
collectively invested to find other civili-
zations, to touch God, further and further,
to dwell in the spirit of divinity!

AmeRícan,   yes, for now, for i love this, my second
land, and i dream to take the accent from
the altercation, and be proud to call
myself american, in the u.s. sense of the
word, AmeRícan, America!